TRAGEDY AT THE TRIANGLE

TRAGEDY AT THE TRIANGLE

FRIENDSHIP IN THE TENEMENTS AND THE SHIRTWAIST FACTORY FIRE

MARY KATE DOMAN

THE
History
PRESS

Published by The History Press
Charleston, SC 29403
www.historypress.net

Front cover: Two girls. *Courtesy of the Library of Congress.*

First published 2015

Manufactured in the United States

ISBN 978.1.62619.645.2

Library of Congress Control Number: 2014954845

Dedicated to Patricia Murphy Doman for teaching me how to be a mom,

and

Tess Murphy Nolan for making me a mom.

CONTENTS

MOVING DAY

Cecelia Napoli ran her hand along the smooth banister as she raced up the twenty-five steps that took her to the front door of her new home. "I love this place already," she said out loud to no one in particular while staring up at the tin ceiling. Even though the lighting was dim, she could make out the small floral patterns etched into the ceiling. Cecelia thought it was beautiful.

The Napoli family had just moved to East Seventh Street on the Lower East Side of Manhattan. The neighborhood was filled with emigrants who came from countries all over the world. Most of them, like Cecelia's family, had come to America to build better lives for themselves.

"I will work hard to make sure my family has an even better life in America than we did in Italy," Cecelia had heard her father say over and over again.

The Napolis were once a very prominent family in Italy. But after a fire burned down the vineyard where they lived and worked, they lost everything. They had no choice but to pack up the few belongings that had not been lost in the fire and start over again. Everyone always said there were plenty of opportunities to make it big in America, so the Napolis sold the last of the wine that had not been lost in the fire. They had just enough money to buy six tickets on the next passenger ship that sailed from Naples to New York. It had all happened so fast.

"I never had a chance to say goodbye to my best friend, Gemma," Cecelia told her mother as the massive ship pulled away from the dock.

"Maybe you will see her again one day," her mother had said. "Maybe Gemma and her family will move to America one day, too."

Cecelia and her mother, Lucia; her father, Lorenzo; and her three younger brothers, Armond, Marco and Leo, had immigrated to America in 1908. Sometimes it was hard for Cecelia to believe that she had been in America for almost three years, and other times it seemed like she had always lived here. When she arrived, Cecelia was homesick for her friends and the sights, smells and sounds of her tiny village back in Italy.

"I wish we never came to America," Cecelia said to her mother.

"Don't say that, Cecilia. We are lucky we had enough money to even pay for our passage to America. You will learn to love it here, maybe even just as much as you love Italy," her mother replied.

At first, Cecelia found the streets of Manhattan scary and confusing. The neighborhood she lived in, the Lower East Side, was packed with over seven hundred people per acre, making it the most crowded neighborhood in the world. To make things even more unsettling, it was filled with people who spoke foreign languages, wore strange clothes and ate exotic foods.

Over time, Cecelia realized that her mother was right.

"Manhattan is exciting," she mused.

Cecelia quickly became used to the different ways of life bustling around her, and she learned to speak English. Cecilia liked hearing all of the different accents and smelling the myriad smells of foreign cuisine. It made her feel alive. She never told this to her parents, though. They wanted her to associate only with other Italian people.

Once, Cecelia told her mother, "I don't know why we even moved to America if I am not allowed to be friends with other girls on my street just because they were born in Germany or Russia or Ireland."

Cecelia's mother looked at her, shook her head and said, "You better not let your father hear you talking like that."

Cecelia knew that most immigrant groups stuck with their own kind.

"Why do I need to learn English?" Cecelia heard her father ask many times. "Everyone I know is Italian. I don't want to talk to anybody who cannot speak Italian."

Even though she loved everything about being Italian, including her mother's cooking and her father's stories about growing up on the family vineyard, Cecilia could not help thinking, "I don't think there is anything wrong with being friends with girls who are Irish, Greek, Russian or Jewish. I am a real American now. Aren't Americans supposed to get along with everybody? Doesn't Lady Liberty welcome everyone to America the same way when they first arrive at Ellis Island?"

However, today Cecelia was not going to let her parents' opinions get her down. Today was the day they were finally moving into their new home. Ever since they moved to America, Cecelia and her family had lived with her Uncle Carlo and two cousins in a two-room tenement around the corner on Orchard Street. Even though Cecelia's father had a good job as a wine merchant, he worked very hard six, sometimes seven, days a week to save up enough money to move his family to their own tenement apartment.

Lucia was always saying, "You work too hard, Lorenzo. You need to relax. Take a day off and play with the children every once in a while."

"Hard work is the only thing that is going to help us achieve our American dream. The first part of our American dream is to rent our own apartment, and renting a decent apartment costs money, so I have to work as much as I can. I don't have time to relax," Lorenzo replied every time.

THE NAPOLIS' NEW HOME was bigger than the one they lived in with Cecelia's uncle and cousins. With three fewer people living under the same roof, there would be much more room for playing, eating and sleeping, too. On Orchard Street, Cecelia had slept on a small cot in the kitchen, and her parents shared the tiny bedroom with Uncle Carlo. Her brothers and cousins slept in the front room with their bodies lying across wooden crates and their heads resting on the couch instead of on pillows. It was the only place that could accommodate the boys' lanky bodies.

Unlike the Orchard Street tenement, not all of the other families who lived on East Seventh Street were from Italy. Cecelia could not believe her parents would move into a building so diverse, but as more people came to the Lower East Side, housing options were becoming increasingly harder to find, as well as more expensive.

"We'll just stay here until something opens up in an all-Italian building," Cecelia overheard her father tell Uncle Carlo while they were lugging their suitcases and their few pieces of furniture up the stairs to the fifth floor.

Once again, Cecelia would be sleeping on a cot in the kitchen, but she didn't mind. The kitchen in their new apartment was much nicer than the one in Uncle

Carlo's. It had a sink, a coal-burning stove and a little cutout that looked into the front room. It even had lights that turned on when you put a penny in the little slot next to the front door. Cecelia hoped that her father would keep on making enough money to keep the lights on all of the time. She had heard stories about some families not being able to use their lights when money was tight. "I can't imagine having a luxury like lights and not being able to use them," Cecelia said to her youngest brother, Leo.

"I know," Leo replied, "I wish we could keep them on all the time—even while we're sleeping!"

THE COT CECELIA USED for a bed was in the corner next to the stove. She lay down on it, thinking about how far her family had come from the little Italian village where she was born. "If only Gemma could see me now," Cecelia thought. "We have lights and a stove, and I speak English as well as I speak Italian." Just then, Cecelia heard muffled voices coming from the apartment below. She got off her cot and put her left ear to the dime-sized space that ran between the planks that made up the wood floor. She heard everything they were saying, but she could not understand the language they spoke. "They aren't speaking English...or Italian. Hmm. I think the bagel peddlers speak like that. I bet they're speaking in Yiddish," Cecelia noticed. "They must be Jewish."

Cecelia placed an eye to the space in the floor between the wood planks and peered into the room downstairs. She saw a girl about her age talking with a woman Cecilia assumed was the girl's mother. They both had long brown hair and were wearing identical black long-sleeved dresses. Cecilia listened to them talking for a few minutes. Even though she did not know what they were saying to each other, Cecilia got the feeling that they were talking about her family's arrival at the tenement. After a few minutes, the girl's mother walked out of Cecilia's view. She heard noises coming from their stove.

"She must be starting dinner," Cecilia thought.

The girl pulled a small red rubber ball and ten silver jacks from her pocket. She squatted down, scattered the jacks on the ground in front of her, bounced the ball and scooped up the jacks one by one while the ball was in the air. As Cecilia was watching the girl pick up the last jack, Armond, Marco and Leo burst into the room with the last of the Napolis' belongings. The noise startled the girl below. She looked up and saw Cecelia's eye staring at her.

"What are you looking at?" the girl yelled up to her in perfect English.

Cecelia quickly jumped up.

"Who *is* that girl?" she wondered as she walked through the kitchen to join the rest of her family in the front room.

"Help your mother set the table," Lorenzo said to Cecelia in Italian.

"Yes, father," replied Cecelia. "Have you met any of our neighbors yet?" she asked.

"Oh, yes," smiled Lorenzo. "The Rossis live on the second floor and the Marinos live on the fourth floor."

"Do any of them have any girls who are my age?" Cecelia asked her father.

"No, Cecelia they do not. The Rossis do not have any children, and the Marinos have two little girls," he told her. "I am sorry, Cecelia. You always seem to be the only girl your age wherever we go."

"Not when we lived in Italy," said Cecelia. "In Italy, I had Gemma to play with."

"You'll make a new friend," Cecelia's mother chimed in. "There are hundreds of Italian families living on East Seventh Street. You will find a new best friend soon."

As Cecelia helped her mother finish setting the table, she thought to herself, "I know I'll find a new best friend soon, but I don't think she's going to be Italian."

LUCIA MADE HER FAMILY a special dinner of homemade pasta, warm bread and fresh, soft cheeses.

"This dinner is the start of the next chapter in the Napoli family story," said Lorenzo as he sat at the head of the table smiling proudly at his wife and children. "We have our own apartment, I have a good job and we are all healthy. We are well on our way to making the Napoli family American dream come true."

Cecilia smiled back at her father.

"Even though we don't always see eye to eye," she thought, "we both share the same American dream."

Without waiting for her parents to ask, Cecelia cleared the table. As the only daughter, she was expected to help her mother by cleaning and taking care of her brothers. Cecelia dreamed of becoming a teacher after graduating from high school so that she could make her own money, but she knew that was a very lofty goal for an immigrant girl.

"When I'm a teacher, I'm going to give most of my money to Father so we can eat homemade pasta, fresh vegetables and just-caught fish every night," Cecelia thought. "I will also ask him to use the money I make to keep the lights in the apartment on all night for Leo, and I'll buy myself a nice, crisp shirtwaist and long wool skirt—like the fancy ladies wear in Washington Square Park."

Cecelia smiled and laughed to herself. "I know it will never happen, but it's nice to have my own secret American dream, too," she thought.

"Quit daydreaming, Cecelia—come and help me give your brothers a bath," Cecelia's mother yelled from the sink in the kitchen. "The water should be warm enough now. Go and fetch it off the stove for me."

Cecelia helped her mother bathe and put Marco and Leo to bed. Armond decided that since he was eight, he didn't need their help anymore, so he washed up and put himself to bed as Cecilia heated some more water on the stove and cleaned herself up. Then she knelt down beside her cot, brought her hands together and started her nightly prayers. First Cecelia recited the Hail Mary and the Our Father, and then she quietly added, "God bless Mother and Father, Armond, Marco and Leo, all of my family and friends back in Italy, especially Gemma, Uncle Carlo and all of my cousins in America. Please keep us all safe, and help us make our American dreams come true."

Just before climbing into bed, Cecelia thought she saw something scurry across the floor. "What's that?" she gasped as it flickered again. At first she thought it was one of the mice she had seen in the hallway earlier, but as Cecilia looked closer, she saw that it wasn't a mouse at all. It was a big brown eye, and it was staring right at her. Cecilia instantly knew that the eye belonged to the girl she had seen playing Jacks earlier.

"Hello. What's your name?" Cecilia whispered so that she wouldn't wake up her family.

"Rose," the girl with the peering eye said.

Before Cecelia could get another word in, Rose blurted out, "Meet me on the fourth-floor landing tomorrow morning at seven o'clock sharp. I have to go before my parents hear me." Rose jumped down from the chair that she was standing on and moved it a few feet to the right.

"Don't forget, fourth floor, seven o'clock!" murmured Rose as she got into her cot one floor below Cecelia.

"I wouldn't dare forget," Cecelia thought as she crawled into her own cot feeling both exhausted and excited.

"I wouldn't miss it for anything."

Cecilia smiled as she closed her eyes. She already loved living in her tenement on East Seventh Street.

2

THE GIRL DOWNSTAIRS

Even though her new apartment was still quiet and dark, when Cecilia awoke at six o'clock, she could not fall back to sleep. Outside, East Seventh Street was waking up. Peddlers set up their pushcarts as they readied for a day of selling everything from tin cups to tulips to tomatoes. Every day, thousands of pushcart peddlers walked the streets of the Lower East Side, shouting out the names of the goods they offered in their native languages. This Sunday morning was no exception.

One of Cecelia's favorite things to do was to walk up and down the streets looking at what the men and women had to offer.

"It's just like back in Italy," Cecelia reflected. "You can buy anything you can think of, all in one place."

Cecelia picked up a few lumps of coal from a metal bucket on the floor and placed them on top of the burning embers in the stove. Then she moved the heavy iron teapot to the front burner, filled it up with water and waited for it to boil.

"Only thirty minutes until I get to meet Rose," she thought. "I have never really met a Jewish person before. I wonder if she will like me."

Cecelia's mind wandered back to Italy and to all of the fun times she had shared with Gemma. Gemma and her family lived on the vineyard next to the Napolis'. The two girls used to spend their days playing school, sewing clothes for their dolls, running through the cobblestone streets of their village and sleeping under the stars on warm summer nights. Those nights were always Cecelia's favorite. She always believed that the vines that blanketed the vineyard protected them from danger. Cecelia and Gemma fell asleep talking and giggling about their day and the people in the village. How she ached to have a friend like that again.

The teapot's sudden whistle snapped Cecelia back to the present. She smiled as her mother strode into the kitchen.

"*Buongiorno*, Cecelia," Lucia said.

"Good morning to you, too, mother. The water is ready. I'll make some oatmeal for the boys," replied Cecelia.

"You are a good girl, Cecelia. Always such a good helper. I don't know how we'd get along without you," her mother said in Italian.

Cecilia went into the front room to wake up her sleeping brothers, but first she stopped and peered out of the only window in the whole apartment. It looked out to the street five stories below. The sun was shining, and there wasn't a cloud in the sky. It was a beautiful September day. Once again, Cecilia thought about how lucky she was to live in such a wonderful and lively place.

Cecilia looked over at her brothers and smiled. "Wake up! Your breakfast is ready. It's beautiful outside. Once you are finished eating, you can go outside and play before we have to go to church. Hurry up!"

The three boys picked their heads up off the couch and looked sleepily at their older sister. One by one, they slowly rose from their makeshift beds and stacked their crates in the corner. The front room transformed from their bedroom back into the living room once again.

Cecelia and her mother set the table as the boys sat around it. They gobbled down their breakfast without looking up.

"Come over and have some oatmeal," Cecelia called out to her father, who was bent over in the kitchen tying his work boots.

"I don't have time this morning, Cecelia," he said. "I can't be late for work today. I have to go down to the docks to pick up wine for the store. I will see you tonight when I get home. This is a new responsibility Mr. Costa gave me. I can't mess it up."

Lorenzo stood up, blew a kiss goodbye to his wife and daughter and walked out the front door with his three boys at his heels.

"Be at Saint Anthony's in time for nine o'clock Mass," Lucia yelled after them.

"He works so hard for our family," Lucia told Cecilia. "Even though he has to miss church when he works on a Sunday, your father is very fortunate to have met Mr. Costa. I don't know what he would do for work if he did not have a job selling wine at his shop."

Cecelia glanced at the clock above the stove. It was six forty-five.

"Only fifteen more minutes until I meet Rose. I don't know if Mother will let me be friends with a Jewish girl. How can I meet her without letting Mother know?" she wondered. "I'll just tell her that I'm exploring the building. That way I won't really be lying."

Cecelia quickly got dressed and informed her mother of her plans to explore the building.

"Remember, we're leaving for church at eight thirty. Don't be late," her mother warned.

When Cecelia stepped onto the fourth-floor landing at seven o'clock on the dot, she found Rose waiting for her.

"Hi," Cecelia started shyly.

"Hello, how old are you?" Rose asked. "I just turned fifteen."

"Me too," Cecelia answered.

"Do you go to school or do you work?" Rose continued.

"School," Cecelia smiled. "I want to be a teacher someday."

"I used to go to school, but now I have to work to make money so I can help my family. My papa used to be a tailor. He worked at Lord and Taylor making dresses for all of the rich ladies on Fifth Avenue. But a few months ago, he started losing his eyesight. He couldn't sew as well as he used to, and he got fired. Since it is only Papa, Mama and me, and Mama does not know how to speak English, I had to quit school and get a job. I work at a garment factory called the Triangle Waist Company, but most people call it the Triangle Shirtwaist Factory. I'm a finisher. I sew buttons onto the shirts," explained Rose.

As Rose was talking, the smile faded from Cecelia's face. "Oh Rose, I'm so sorry. I couldn't imagine having to work at a factory."

"Don't be sorry," Rose proudly replied. "I actually like working. I'm glad that I can help my family, and the Triangle Shirtwaist Factory isn't such a bad place. I make nine dollars a week. I do miss school, though. I really liked learning."

"Wow, nine dollars a week is a lot of money. It's almost as much as my father makes at the wine store," Cecelia acknowledged. "It's nice that you're able to help your family. I've heard of the Triangle Shirtwaist Factory, and I love shirtwaists. If you have to work in a factory, I guess it's best to work at one that makes nice things."

"Oh yes, that's one of the reasons why I don't mind it too much. Thank goodness Papa taught me how to sew when I was young. When he first lost his job, we didn't know what we were going to do." Rose continued. "We thought that we would be evicted. But some of Mama's friends from our synagogue work at the Triangle Waist Company, and they told their boss how good I sew. He gave me a chance, and now I am one of the youngest girls at the factory."

"That was very nice of him," said Cecelia. "It sounds like a very good job. I like sewing, too. When I was younger, I used to make clothes for my doll. Now I help my mother fix my brothers' clothes when they rip them, which is all of the time. I am sure I'm not as good as you though."

"Well I do have a lot of practice," smiled Rose. "And now I make enough money to pay rent here and buy food for my family to eat all week, as well as have a nice Shabbos meal."

Cecilia looked at Rose quizzically. "What's a Shabbos meal?" she asked.

"That's right," Rose laughed. "I almost forgot. You're not Jewish. Shabbos is the Yiddish word for our Sabbath day, which lasts from sundown on Friday evenings to sundown on Saturday evenings. Every week we begin our Shabbos with a meal filled with prayers and candle lightings. I was helping Mama put away our Shabbos candles last night when you saw me through the gaps in your floor. The silver candlestick holders have been in our family since before my grandparents were born. My mother brought them from Russia when she moved here as a young girl. We light them every Shabbos."

Rose described the Shabbos dinner to Cecelia as a family celebration to begin a day of rest. "We're not supposed to work at all on Saturdays—we're not even supposed to cook or turn on the lights, but I have to work at the factory or I will lose my job. So I really enjoy the Shabbos dinner since I can't be with my family on Saturday.

"Every Friday, eighteen minutes before sunset, Mama lights two candles. Then we sing together, and Papa blesses the wine and the challah. Challah is a special bread that we eat every Friday and on holidays. She bakes it and prepares the rest of the dinner for us. There is usually a lot of food. It takes her all day to prepare and cook."

"That sounds nice," said Cecelia. "I'm sure you know that I'm Catholic. I was born in Italy, and most Italians are Catholic. We moved here almost two years ago. We used to live with my uncle on Orchard Street. Mostly Italians lived there, and there aren't any Jewish girls who go to my school, so you're the first Jewish girl I have ever spent any real time with."

"I didn't meet anyone Catholic or Italian until I started working at the factory," Rose recalled. "I work with a lot of Italian girls, but we aren't allowed to talk to each other while we work, so I don't have any friends at the factory."

"Well, I'll be your first Italian friend," Cecelia said. "I haven't had a friend since I moved to America. It will be nice to have someone to spend time with who lives so close to me."

"I work a lot, but most of the time I'm at work, you're at school. Maybe we can meet at night and you can teach me what you learned at school that day?" suggested Rose.

Cecelia thought about how nice it would be not only to have a new friend but to be able to help her out as well.

"That's a great idea!" Cecelia exclaimed. "I used to play school with my best friend back in Italy all of the time. Now, I'll get to play school for real. It will be good practice for when I become a teacher."

"There is an old storage closet in the basement by the back door," Rose told Cecelia. "I don't think that anyone uses it anymore. We can clean it up and make it our classroom."

"Can we go and look at it now?" asked Cecelia. "I still have a little bit of time before I have to go to church."

The two girls bounded down the tenement staircase giggling and holding hands.

"This is perfect!" Cecelia exclaimed after they stepped into the storage closet. "It's about the same size as my parents' bedroom. We have some extra crates that we used for moving. Mother was going to throw them out because they take up so much room, but they'd be perfect for us to use for chairs and desks."

Rose pointed to the broken assortment of discarded old household items and dirty rags scattered on the closet floor. "I'll clean up this mess while you're at your church today. We can meet back here tomorrow at seven o'clock for my first lesson!"

Both girls smiled at each other, and then Cecelia threw her arms around Rose and gave her a hug. "Thank you," she said.

"I should be thanking you," Rose countered. "You're the one who is going to be helping me."

"Yes, but if you hadn't invited me to meet you this morning, I still wouldn't have made a new friend today," said Cecelia.

"Cecelia! Time to go to church," a voice from upstairs sang out in Italian.

"That's my mother," Cecelia told Rose. "I have to go, but I will meet you back here tomorrow."

"OK. I will see you then," Rose happily declared as she waved goodbye to Cecelia.

Cecelia sat in between her mother and Leo in a pew at Saint Anthony of Padua Church. She had done this every Sunday since the Napolis had moved to New York. She looked up at the gilded cathedral ceiling and colorful stained-glass windows that depicted the lives of several saints and the holy family. Saint Anthony's was a beautiful church. Father Louis, who welcomed his congregation in Italian, sang along with the loud music piping out of the new organ that was perched way up in the rafters. Cecelia usually loved Mass and paid rapt attention to the music, readings and Father Louis's words, but today she found her mind wandering.

Cecelia could not stop thinking about her new friend and daydreaming about all of the adventures they would share together.

Later that night, Cecelia knelt down next to her cot to say her prayers. Through the floorboards, she saw the lights go out in the Mehls' apartment. Even though Rose was not Catholic, Cecelia added her name to the litany of family and friends she prayed for each evening.

"Good night, my friend," Cecelia whispered to the darkness. "See you tomorrow."

3

HAPPY TIMES TO
HARD TIMES

For nearly three months, Cecilia and Rose met in the old storage closet every day except for Fridays, when Rose had her Shabbos dinner. The girls grew very close, but neither one of their families knew they were friends. They knew that their families just wouldn't understand their unlikely friendship, so they vowed to keep it a secret.

"I'm afraid my father will tell me I'm not allowed to be friends with a Jewish girl," Cecilia confessed.

"And I don't think that my papa will let me be friends with an Italian girl," Rose added.

"It will be our secret then," reasoned Cecilia.

Each girl told her parents that she had turned the closet into a reading space for herself. No one bothered them, since no one else ever needed to go down into the basement. Even Cecilia's brothers kept away.

"Why would I want to go to a reading room?" Armond asked after Cecilia asked him to stay away so she could read in peace.

Cecilia looked forward to her time with Rose more than anything else since moving to New York. The girls giggled about the other people who lived in their tenement, and Cecelia taught Rose things like percents and poetry.

Soon, Cecelia began to loathe Friday nights. Besides not being able to spend time with Rose, she couldn't help but be a little jealous of her Shabbos dinner as the delicious smells of fresh challah, fish and beef wafted up through the floorboards. Though they ate well, the Napolis never had such an elaborate meal.

"Another reason to be glad we're not Jewish," Cecelia overheard her father complain to her mother one Friday night. "All of that food they eat every Friday costs a lot of money. We wouldn't be able to have a fancy dinner like that every week. I see that girl of theirs go off to work every day in a factory. She is about the same age as Cecelia. She should be in school, not forced to work so they can have nice meals."

"That's not a very nice thing to say, Lorenzo," her mother chided. "We should count our blessings that you have a good job. Many girls Cecelia's age have to work to help their families. Mind your own business. You have enough things to worry about, like staying healthy enough to work six days a week so that you can provide for our family."

Her mother was right. Her father did not know the Mehls' circumstances. Cecelia thought he was only criticizing them because they were Jewish. Cecelia had to bite her tongue or else she would have defended the Mehls and told them about Mr. Mehl's poor eyesight. She couldn't do that or her parents would find out about her secret friendship. Cecelia now knew for certain that her father would put an end to the friendship if he ever found out about it.

One cold November evening, Cecelia and Rose were in their storage room going over some poetry when they heard a woman sobbing. The crying seemed to be coming from the hallway. The woman spoke in Italian between her cries.

"That's Mrs. Marino," Cecelia told Rose. "She's so upset even I can't understand what she is saying."

"Come on, let's get closer so we can find out what happened," Rose suggested.

The girls made their way to the stairwell and hid below the first-floor landing. It looked like all of the Marinos' belongings had been tossed into the street.

Lucia joined Mrs. Marino by the front door of the tenement building. She held the distressed woman in her arms.

"I don't know what we are going to do," Mrs. Marino stammered. "We told the landlord yesterday that Nicoli lost his job so we would be a little late with November's rent, and today they threw us out. I just came home from trying to find another housecleaning job. The landlord had someone come and throw all of our things out of the building while I was gone."

Mrs. Marino looked down at the brown and red paisley scarf she held in her hands. It had a big tear down the center. "My mother gave me this scarf before I left Italy. It has been passed down to the women in my family for many generations. Look, now it is ruined," she sniffled.

Cecelia did not have to translate Mrs. Marino's words for Rose. Even without understanding Italian, Rose knew that the Marinos had been evicted from their home because they could not afford the rent anymore.

The two girls looked at each other and shook their heads. "What are they going to do?" Rose wondered. "Her two little girls are too young to work, and cleaning a few houses won't be enough for them to make rent anywhere."

Lucia and Mrs. Marino began picking up the clothes and furnishings that were strewn across the stairs and sidewalk, placing them in a pile in front of the tenement.

"I knew our landlord was mean, but I never thought he would throw us out on the street," said Mrs. Marino as she picked up one of her daughters' tattered dolls. "We can stay with my sister and her family until we figure out what to do. Her apartment is already overcrowded, but we do not have anywhere else to go. At least her tenement does not have any Jews living in it."

From her hiding place, Cecelia winced at Mrs. Marino's last remark. Noticing Cecelia flinch, Rose asked her what happened.

Mrs. Marino's words made Cecelia feel awful. She didn't want to hurt Rose's feelings by repeating Mrs. Marino's callous words. So she left out the part about being happy to live in a building without any Jewish people when she relayed the exchange between Mrs. Marino and her mother to Rose.

"Such a shame," Rose acknowledged. "She seems like a nice woman. I hope her husband finds another job very soon."

Rose's sympathy for the Marinos made Cecelia even more unsettled.

"I am sure they will be fine. Come on, let's finish our poetry lesson," Cecelia insisted as she stuck her tongue out in Mrs. Marino's direction. The tiny gesture made Cecelia lose her footing for a second, and she grabbed the rickety banister to steady herself. As she steadied herself, Cecelia thought she saw her mother glance at her and Rose together just before they ducked out of sight.

"I hope Mother did not see me with Rose," Cecelia thought. "I guess I'll find out later."

Lucia did not mention anything to Cecelia about seeing her on the stairs with Rose. Cecelia was relieved, but she did find it strange that her mother asked about her schoolwork.

"I hope you're keeping up with your studies and not getting into any mischief," she said with a knowing smile. "You are going to need to work hard if you're to become a teacher."

"Oh, I am, Mother. I'm working harder at my studies than I ever have before," Cecelia promised.

"I thought as much," Lucia remarked.

It was the truth. Cecelia had never had higher marks in school. By teaching Rose everything she learned in school, Cecelia had become one of the top students in her class.

Cecelia spent the rest of November and the beginning of December much like she had spent the early fall. She replicated her teacher's history, arithmetic and English lessons in the makeshift classroom. Cecelia proved to be a great teacher. As each day passed and the daylight of the late autumn grew shorter and shorter, she became a more efficient teacher as well. Rose excelled in both history and English. She did not particularly like arithmetic, but she knew she needed it to help her with sewing. Excelling at fractions and measurements would help Rose become a sewing machine operator faster. More money would come along with the promotion, too. Rose figured that with Cecelia's help, she could reach her goal sometime in the spring.

THE GIRLS' TIME TOGETHER was not filled only with work; they also sang songs and played Jacks and cards together. One of their favorite card games was Snap, which they spent many hours playing.

By mid-December, the Mehls began preparing for Hanukkah while the Napolis got ready for Christmas. Like the weekly Shabbos meal, Hanukkah was filled with religious traditions and meals. Both girls told each other about their different holiday customs. Since small gifts are usually given to family and friends for both holidays, Cecelia and Rose decided to exchange gifts.

"Hanukkah starts after Christmas this year, so let's give each other our gifts the night before Christmas," Rose suggested.

"Good idea," said Cecelia. "That will give us a week to get each other a present."

After an hour of singing the Christmas carols that she had taught Rose, Cecelia went upstairs to her apartment. Her father arrived home from work shortly after his daughter.

"Are we getting a Christmas tree this year?" Cecelia asked him.

"Of course we are, my *amore!*" Lorenzo replied. "I'll even let you pick it out."

Cecelia smiled. It was the third Christmas they were celebrating in America, and for the first time since leaving Italy, everything in her life felt perfect. She felt like she was living the American dream her father often spoke about.

"Cecelia, I almost forgot. Look what I have for you!" her father exclaimed. "It was in our mailbox."

Lorenzo handed Cecelia a thin cream-colored envelope. Cecelia noticed the handwriting on the front right away.

"It's from Gemma!" Cecelia cried. It had been months since she had heard from her old friend back in Italy. Cecelia realized that she could not remember the last time she had thought about Gemma. Her days were filled with school and Rose. This realization made Cecelia both happy and sad. She tore open the envelope and carefully pulled out the letter from inside. As Cecelia read her friend's words, she felt the once familiar feeling of missing her old home. This time, though, she noticed that the pain was not as sharp. It had dulled just like her mother had said it would.

"That's because America really is my home now," she thought.

"Gemma sends her love and wishes everyone a very Merry Christmas," Cecelia told her family.

Lorenzo hugged his daughter and said, "You will find a friend like Gemma again. Good friends are hard to come by, but once you find one, you will be friends forever."

Cecelia hugged her father back. "I know," she told him.

In the doorway of the front room, Lucia looked at her husband and daughter with a knowing smile. "Come on, you two, dinner is ready. Time to eat."

"Ah, supper! My favorite time of the day," teased Lorenzo as he made his way to the table where the three boys were already sitting.

Lorenzo sat down, too, and raised his glass. "I want to make a toast," he said. "To our American dream." But before he took a sip of his wine, Lorenzo coughed.

"I hope you're not getting sick," Lucia said. "You don't want to spend Christmas in bed!"

"Don't worry, Lucia. I'm as strong as an ox. It's probably just a cold. I'll fight it off," Lorenzo reassured her, "Now, about that Christmas tree, Cecelia. Let's get one tonight!"

After dinner, they did just that.

"HURRY UP, OPEN IT!" Rose squeaked excitedly as Cecelia unwrapped the gift she had given her. It was wrapped in newspaper and tied with one of the ribbons that usually adorned Rose's hair. "I hope you like it."

Cecelia carefully removed the paper to find a bound journal with her initials, "C.N.," etched into the cover.

"Oh, Rose, it's beautiful," Cecelia marveled. "This is the nicest gift that anyone's ever given me. I can't thank you enough."

"You thank me every time you teach me something new," Rose beamed. "Fill it with your favorite stories, quotes and poems."

"I will treasure it always. Now open your present," Cecelia playfully ordered.

Cecelia smiled as Rose ripped the pretty paper off the used copy of Shakespearian sonnets she had won by coming in first place in a spelling bee at school.

"Now you can read Shakespeare every night," beamed Cecelia.

"This is the first book that is truly mine. Thank you, Cecelia. I love it. I really love it," Rose promised as she stood up to give Cecelia a hug.

But before she could reach her friend, the door to the closet burst open and in burst Armond. Both girls jumped back in surprise. Cecelia thought Armond was going to be mad at her for spending time with Rose, but he didn't even seem to notice Rose standing there.

"Cecelia, come quick!" he demanded. "Something has happened to Father!"

Cecelia followed her brother up the stairs to the fifth floor. "Where's Mother?" she asked.

"She ran out of butter when she was making Christmas Eve dinner. So she went out to buy some more. A few minutes later, Father came out of their room and couldn't stop coughing."

As soon as she entered the apartment, Cecelia knew something was terribly wrong. Her father was lying across the couch in the front room. His face was as white as a sheet. He was covered in sweat, and it looked as though he was having trouble breathing.

"Father!" Cecelia gasped.

Lorenzo tried to speak to his daughter, but he choked on a cough instead. It hurt Cecelia to even look at him. Her three younger brothers stood paralyzed at her side.

"His cough is really bad," Cecelia thought. "I hope it's not consumption."

She hesitated for a moment, but then she sprung into action. "Marco and Leo," she commanded, "run over to Orchard Street and fetch Dr. Oliveri. You remember him. He lives next door to Uncle Carlo—hurry! Get there and back as fast as you can!"

The two youngest Napolis sprinted down the stairs and into the cold winter night without a word.

"Armond, help me move Father into his bed," directed Cecelia.

They each put one arm around their father's waist and neck as they carefully helped him walk from the front room, through the kitchen and into the room he shared with Lucia.

"He is very weak," Armond said after they had laid him down on his bed.

"And light," noted Cecelia. "He's lost a lot of weight. Let's pray that he doesn't have consumption."

Armond nodded his head, and the two siblings said a silent prayer for their father.

Marco and Leo arrived with Dr. Oliveri in tow at the same moment Lucia came home.

When she realized what was happening, Lucia screamed, dropped the butter and ran to her husband's side.

"Lorenzo!" she cried as she stroked his sweat-soaked cheek. "Please be OK. Please be OK," Lucia pleaded over and over.

Lorenzo tried to smile at her, but this only made him cough uncontrollably once again. Dr. Oliveri ushered Lucia out of the room.

"Stay out here with your children while I examine him," he said. "I'll have a better idea of what's wrong in a few minutes, but I have to warn you Lucia, it does not look good."

Lucia did as the doctor told her without a fight. She grabbed her children and hugged them tight.

"He will be all right," she said. "It will be all right," she choked through her tears.

The doctor emerged a short time later. "I am sorry, Lucia," he said. "Lorenzo has consumption. We've caught it early, but he must be taken to a sanatorium as soon as possible. He needs to be cared for by the doctors there, get plenty of rest and breathe lots of fresh air. There is a sanatorium just north of Manhattan on Hart Island. I have a few colleagues who work there; I'll go ahead and let them know Lorenzo is coming. I will send some men to fetch him in the morning."

After Dr. Oliveri left the Napolis' apartment, it seemed quiet and cold. All of the Christmas excitement that had been lingering in the air for the past week disappeared.

"He must have caught tuberculosis from one of the dock workers who unloads the wine for the shop," Lucia considered. "Consumption is bad on those ships. I thought by working in the store most of the time he wouldn't contract it. I guess I was wrong."

A few hours later, Cecelia lay in bed wondering, "How could everything be so right one moment and so wrong the next? This is not how our American dream was supposed to turn out. With Father at a sanatorium, how are we supposed to get enough money to eat and pay rent each month?" Cecelia was too exhausted to come up with an answer right then. She pulled the covers over her eyes and cried herself to sleep.

Very early the next morning, two men dressed all in white came for Lorenzo. Cecelia could not help but think that it should have been Santa Claus, not orderlies, paying them a visit. They picked up her father without saying a word.

Everyone in the tenement, including Rose, watched as they carried Lorenzo out of the building. Rose tried to catch Cecelia's eye, but she couldn't even look at her friend. Her heart hurt too much.

4

FACTORY DAYS

A lone in the storage room where she had shared so many wonderful hours with Rose, Cecelia thought about how her life had drastically changed in an instant. It was Christmas Day, and instead of opening presents and singing carols with her brothers, Cecelia and her mother spent the day disinfecting their apartment. Dr. Oliveri had reassured them that if they had not already started showing the signs of consumption, they had most likely not contracted the disease from their father. Just to be safe, though, Lucia decided to clean everything thoroughly anyway. After they had hung the last rag up to dry, Lucia called her daughter into her bedroom.

"Cecelia, I have to talk to you," she said. "You saw what they did to the Marinos when they found out Mr. Marino lost his job. We can't let that happen to us."

"I know, Mother. That is why I have decided to leave school and work in a factory," Cecelia volunteered.

Cecelia's mother looked at her with tears in her eyes.

"Oh, my little love," she sighed. "I'm so sorry this has to happen, but I don't think we have any other options. Your brothers are too young to get jobs that pay decent money, and I won't make enough cleaning houses to cover the rent."

"Don't worry, Mother. I already know where I can get a job," Cecelia reassured her. "I can work as a button finisher for the Triangle Waist Company."

"Is that where your friend Rose from downstairs works?" Lucia inquired.

Cecelia's mouth dropped open. "How do you know about Rose?" she asked.

Her mother shook her head and smiled gently. "Do you think a mother doesn't know how her daughter spends all of her days? "

"And you aren't angry with me?" she mused.

"No, Cecelia, I'm not. Helping someone is always a good thing. I am proud of you. You are a true American. You treat everyone the same no matter what their background," praised Lucia. "You're like a real life Lady Liberty."

Cecelia smiled happily at her mother's compliment. Then she wrinkled her brow, "Does Father know about Rose?" she pressed.

"No. He doesn't. He's very stuck in his ways. He does not trust anyone who is not Italian. But he will be very grateful to Rose for getting you a job," she remarked. "Your father is going to be very upset when he finds out that you have to work in a factory, but there is nothing he can do about it now. At least he'll find some comfort knowing that you already have a friend to look out for you at work. You will be the one to carry on the Napoli family American dream for him."

Now that she was going to work at the Triangle Shirtwaist Factory, Cecelia practiced her sewing skills. She practiced by sewing and resewing the same two buttons onto a swatch of fabric as Rose gave her little pointers.

"You can come with me to work tomorrow," Rose told Cecelia. "I told my forelady, Mrs. Lansner, about you. She said you could start right away so your family won't miss a rent payment."

The abruptness of her new life scared Cecilia. "I'm a bit nervous," she confessed.

"Don't be," Rose quipped. "You're great at sewing now. In fact, you're better than some of the girls who already work there."

On Monday, December 26, Cecelia walked down the stairs to the same landing where she had first met Rose. Cecelia could not believe that their first meeting had been less than four months ago. It seemed like she and Rose had been friends for a lot longer. Rose appeared on the landing a split second after Cecelia. She looked at her friend, and her mouth broke into a grin.

"Come on, working girl," laughed Rose. "You don't want to be late on your first day!" Then she grabbed Cecelia by the hand, and the two girls bounded down the stairs together.

Cold air blasted them as soon as they opened the front door to their tenement building.

"It's much colder at five thirty in the morning than I thought it would be," Cecelia mused. "I've never walked through New York this early before."

"That's because the sun isn't up yet. You'll get used to it quickly, and we'll warm up as we walk," Rose said. "From now on, we won't leave this early. We can leave a half hour later, but Mrs. Lansner wants to meet you before the other workers arrive. We can take our time today so you can walk off some of your first day jitters. The cold air will wake you up. You have to be alert at all times while you're working. One little mistake and you could lose your job, or worse—you could get hurt."

The girls lived almost a mile and a half away from the factory. The walk usually took Rose about a half hour, but today she walked slower and pointed out things to Cecelia along the way. She was already grateful to have a friend with her on the long, cold walk. Rose was so positive that she even made the frigid temperature pleasant.

They took a left out of their tenement on East Seventh Street and Avenue D and walked three blocks west toward Tompkins Square Park. Cecelia loved that park and quietly thought about the many times she had accompanied her brothers there to run and play in the grass after school. She sighed heavily at the realization that those carefree days were now over for her. Upon hearing Cecelia's burdened sigh, Rose put her arm around her friend's shoulder and pulled her into a hug.

"Things are different for you now, but you will be happy again, Cecelia. I know it. You'll be a great finisher in the factory. You will make the money to feed and house your family while your father is away. He will get stronger every day and be back home before you know it," Rose assured and comforted her friend.

Cecelia relaxed a little at her friend's kind words. Putting on a brave face and fighting back tears, Cecelia replied, "Thank you, Rose. I don't think I could have done this without you by my side."

They walked the next five blocks in contemplative silence. When the girls reached the Cooper Union building, which was only a few blocks east of the Triangle Shirtwaist Factory, Cecelia stopped dead in her tracks.

"Come on, Cecelia," Rose declared. "We're almost there."

Cecelia stared at a small gathering of women. There were about ten of them, and they all wore picket signs. Cecelia noticed right away that the signs protested women working in garment factories—the exact thing she was about to do.

Rose noticed Cecelia looking at the picketers. "It's OK," she said. "They are there every day. They were the leaders in the big garment strike in 1909, and now they are banned from working in the garment industry."

"But why are they protesting?" Cecelia contemplated. "Didn't Carla Lemlich and the other women in the union get what they wanted? I thought they helped factory workers get better wages, working conditions and hours?"

"The factory owners, including the owners of the Triangle Shirtwaist Factory, did give their workers shorter hours and better pay, but some people still don't think it's enough. They think that factories are still unsafe," Rose remarked, "but the Asch Building the Triangle Waist Company is in is very modern. The two men who own it are there all the time. They told us that since it is made of stone, it's fireproof. We don't have anything to worry about. It's not like those old, dark and rickety garment factories in the tenements where we live. Now come on. You and I both need this job, and we will get in trouble if a forelady sees us talking to the picketers. You don't want to be fired before you even start working, do you?" cautioned Rose.

"No, I certainly do not," Cecelia answered as she followed Rose toward Washington Place. After a few steps, she turned around to look at the picketers one more time. One of them stared at her and pointed to the sign across her chest. It read, "Don't Wait Until It's Too Late—Factory Conditions Are STILL Unsafe!"

The picketers made Cecelia uncomfortable. She quickly turned her head and pushed the sudden feeling of uneasiness down into the pit of her stomach. "Don't be so silly," she told herself. "Thousands of people work in factories every day. Everything will be fine."

The Triangle Shirtwaist Factory was located on the top three floors inside of a ten-story building called the Asch Building on the corner of Washington Place and Greene Street. It was just off the east end of Washington Square Park.

One thing Cecelia already liked about work was the location of the factory. Washington Square Park was very nice, and many of the fancy ladies who lived on Fifth Avenue frequented the park after a day filled with lunch and shopping. As was the fashion, most of these ladies wore shirtwaists like the ones Cecelia would soon be adorning with buttons. All of the modern and independent women of the day wore shirtwaists. They were button-down blouses that could be worn without a jacket and tucked into a long skirt. It made Cecelia happy to think that she would be part of making something so beautiful and popular. Perhaps one day she, too, would own a shirtwaist.

Cecelia looked up at the impressive building in front of her and held her head up high. Little did she know that the course of her life would forever change the minute she stepped foot inside the Asch Building. With her black boots all shined up for her first day of work, Cecelia Napoli entered the grand building and became one of the Triangle Waist Company's youngest workers.

"We work all the way up on the ninth floor. We can take the elevator," Rose told Cecelia as they waited in the hallway for their ride up to their workspaces.

The elevator doors opened, and a man who looked to be in his late twenties was inside. He looked at Cecelia and smiled, "*Bongiorno* girls, going up?" he exclaimed.

"Joseph, this is my friend Cecelia," Rose said. "And Cecelia, this is Joseph. He's my favorite elevator operator."

All three of them smiled at one another.

"Nice to meet you," Cecelia said as she reached to shake Joseph's outstretched hand.

"My name is Joseph Zito," he said with a wink. "It's always nice to meet another Italian. Welcome to the Asch Building, and have a great first day of work."

Cecelia liked him immediately.

Joseph started the elevator and quickly took the girls up to the ninth floor. Throughout the tiny elevator shaft, the elevator's gears squeaked and grinded loudly. When they reached their destination, Joseph opened up the heavy steel grate that led into a very large, open room filled with rows and rows of long wooden tables. Across the length of each table were sewing machines with wooden chairs in front of them. Only a small aisle separated the rows from one another. The space was so small that the chair backs touched one another in between the rows.

After they got off the elevator and said goodbye to Joseph, Cecelia noticed a woman standing in the middle of the room. As she made her way toward them, Rose whispered, "That's our forelady, Mrs. Lansner."

Cecelia introduced herself to her new boss and thanked her for giving her a chance at being a finisher at the Triangle Shirtwaist Factory.

Mrs. Lansner seemed to be all business as she informed Cecelia that the Triangle was a vey busy and productive place with over 240 sewing stations on the ninth floor alone. Cecelia marveled at how cramped the room seemed with only three people in it.

"Wow, it must be very tight in here when everyone is working," Cecelia remarked. Rose tried to nudge her without Mrs. Lansner seeing, but the shrewd forelady had obviously seen her.

"We do our best, Miss Napoli," Mrs. Lansner reproached. "I don't usually hire girls until they turn sixteen, but Rose has vouched for you and informed me of your situation. I am very sorry about your father, but you are here to work. Not play," she went on as she gave both Cecelia and Rose a sideways glance. "I trust that you will work from the second you arrive until the second the sewing machines turn off each evening. If I see any chitchatting, giggling or funny business—you will be let go immediately."

"Oh, yes, Mrs. Lansner. You can count on me. I will be the best finisher you have ever seen," Cecelia promised. "I mean, I'll be as good as Rose. She's already taught me everything she knows!"

Mrs. Lansner couldn't help but chuckle at Cecelia's eagerness. "Well, I sincerely hope so. Now, Rose, go show Cecelia where she can put her coat before everyone else arrives."

Rose pulled Cecelia away from Mrs. Lansner as fast as she could. The cloakroom was just a bunch of hooks behind a partition. Once the girls were out of their forelady's earshot, Rose said, "She's not as scary as she seems. She has to put on a tough act for the bosses, but she is very nice and fair to her workers."

Soon, the sewing machine operators began filing in. Each one took her seat at a sewing station. At 7:00 a.m. sharp, the sewing machines started buzzing and whirling.

As a button finisher, Cecelia was tasked with sewing all of the buttons onto an almost finished shirtwaist. She was expected to sew on hundreds of buttons by hand everyday. After only two hours of work, Cecelia looked around. There were already heaps of almost finished shirtwaists piling up everywhere. She had a lot of buttons left to sew. She better work faster—it was going to be a long day.

By the end of her shift at 6:30 p.m., Cecelia had lost count of how many buttons she had sewn. She guessed that it was somewhere around three hundred, and she knew that Rose had sewn many more than her.

"It will get easier," Rose told Cecelia as they walked home. "You will get faster, and your hands will hurt less each day."

"I hope so," Cecelia said. "I knew that working in a factory was going to be tedious, but I didn't think it was going to be this hard."

The two friends reached their tenement just before seven o'clock. It had been a long day for Cecelia, and she knew she had to do it all over again every day for the foreseeable future.

"I don't know how you had the energy to meet me for school lessons after work," Cecelia confided. "I am exhausted. You must have really wanted to learn."

"I did," said Rose. "And I know that you will want to practice your reading and writing again very soon, too. I know there is more to your American dream than sewing buttons, Cecelia."

Cecelia looked warmly at her friend. "Yes, there is. Even though it seems impossible now, I still want to be a teacher someday."

After the girls said goodnight to each other, they parted ways—each to a warm meal and bed. Though their suppers couldn't have been any more different, pasta for Cecelia and fish for Rose, the two girls couldn't have been more similar.

5
FIRE!

For almost three months to the day, Cecelia and Rose met to walk together at six o'clock in the morning, six days a week. Leaving from what they had come to think of as their landing, the two girls chitchatted and giggled the entire way to their jobs at the factory. Neighbors and peddlers alike laughed and smiled at the unlikely pair. Their happiness was contagious, and after seeing them together so many times, no one seemed to notice or care that the girls were from two different cultures.

They had endured the freezing temperatures and winds of a New York City winter and looked forward to the warmth and sunshine the spring promised. The date was March 25, 1911, and it was a particularly beautiful Saturday morning. The sun was already shining, the sky was a deep blue and there wasn't a cloud in sight.

"Today is perfect," Rose exclaimed. "I wish every day could be this beautiful." Then she did a little twirl to emphasize her delight.

Cecelia smiled and looked affectionately at her friend. "What a long way we've come," she thought. "Just a little while ago I thought that I would never have a friend again. Now, Rose and I are just as close as Gemma and I once were."

"Quit your daydreaming, Cecelia," Rose called. "You're going to make us late."

Cecelia snapped back to reality and took a few quick steps to catch up to Rose.

"I still can't believe that we're both factory girls," she said. "Remember when I used to teach you literature and number games in the old storage closet?"

"Yes, and now your brothers use that same closet to play marbles. I will let them borrow it for a bit, but they must sign an oath to acknowledge that it will always be ours," joked Rose.

The past few months had been both challenging and rewarding for Cecelia. She excelled at her job, made enough money to support her family during her father's long absence and had the added bonus of spending a lot of time with Rose. But Cecelia could not help feeling that something was wrong. She could not figure out why, but a nagging feeling ballooned in the bottom of her stomach every time she stepped into the Asch Building and rode the elevator up to the Triangle Shirtwaist Factory on the ninth floor. Today was no exception. Actually, today the feeling was worse.

"Cecelia, you're being silly," she thought. "What could possibly be wrong on such a beautiful day?" Cecelia blamed her uneasiness on the fact that she really missed both school and her father. She knew working at the factory was her life right now, and there was nothing she could do to change it, but knowing that didn't make her reality any less difficult.

"*Bongiorno!*" Joseph boomed in greeting to the small crowd of factory workers waiting for the elevator.

Joseph pulled a lever. Then the elevator started with a jolt. Since it was almost starting time for the whole building, the elevator stopped on almost every floor. When they arrived on the eighth floor, Cecelia recognized some of the men who got off. Like her, they also worked at the Triangle Shirtwaist Factory. But unlike the ninth floor, the eighth floor did not consist of rows of sewing machines. The eighth floor was where the men cut the patterns for the shirtwaists. Cloth and paper patterns were strewn all over tables and hung on strings across the room. There were also big bins of fabric scraps that were sold to rag dealers who remade them into new pieces of cloth.

When they reached the ninth floor, Cecelia, Rose and a handful of other finishers and sewing machine operators stepped out of the elevator and into the spacious yet crowded room.

"I'm so glad today is Saturday," Rose said. "After you get back from church tomorrow, let's go to a nickelodeon."

"That's a great idea, Rose," agreed Cecelia. "I've always wanted to see a nickelodeon film."

Cecelia and Rose smiled as they put their coats and hats on the hooks and made their way across to their button stations by the row of windows overlooking Greene Street.

Saturday was their favorite day at the factory since it closed a little early, at five o'clock instead of six thirty. With only a ten-hour workday and a full day off on Sunday, the girls became antsy as the day wore on. Their half-hour lunch passed quickly, just giving them enough time to get back into the workroom before Mrs. Lansner locked the heavy steel door behind them so the workers could not sneak out to use the lavatory during working hours. At first it had been hard for her to only go to the bathroom once a day, but as with everything else at the Triangle Shirtwaist Factory, Cecelia had learned to accept it. She worked long and hard, but she could not give up her pay.

Cecelia finished sewing her last button of the week onto a shirtwaist. As she was dropping a piece of thread into a wicker waste bin, she heard shattering glass, and someone behind her yelled, "Fire!"

Cecelia froze and then looked up to see Rose dash to the row of windows in front of them.

Rose looked out of the window. There were already fire engines at the Asch Building. A sense of relief washed over her. But her relief was short-lived. The firemen's ladders could not reach them. They were almost three stories too short.

"No!" screamed Rose. "The firemen can't get to us! They can't help us! Their ladders aren't high enough to reach us! We have to find another way out!" The flames were getting closer. They were trapped.

Cecelia heard the fear in her friend's voice. Then she sprung into action, too.

"The fire escape. Come on, Rose!" Cecelia urged as she pointed to their left.

The two girls, followed by dozens more, ran toward the fire escape. Other workers were already climbing out through the window onto the wobbly old structure. But before Cecelia and Rose got there, they heard Mrs. Lansner call out, "Girls! The fire escape can't hold us all! The elevator—it's our only way out!"

Once again, Rose grabbed Cecelia's hand and led her toward the same elevator that had brought them safely up to the ninth floor only ten hours earlier. The elevator was already overcrowded. There was no room for anyone else. There was nowhere to go, and the workers were panicking. They were pushing one another, stepping over one another, pulling hair and clawing at the girls closest to the elevator shaft. Everyone was desperately trying to get into the packed elevator before its doors closed. A girl Cecelia recognized as a sewing machine operator named Jennie got on the elevator right in front of her. She was the last person who could fit inside.

But just then, Jennie fainted and fell back into the crowd of terrified factory workers behind her. Before Cecelia could even register what was happening, she felt a strong and deliberate push from behind.

"What's happening?" Cecelia thought, as she caught herself and fell forward. She was now standing in the same spot that had been occupied by Jennie only seconds ago.

Cecelia quickly turned around and saw Rose standing there with her arms still outstretched from the shove she had given Cecelia.

"Go, live your American dream—for both of us," Rose sputtered to Cecelia as the elevator shut its doors and began its descent.

The ride down to safety and away from the flames felt like an eternity. Everyone was pushed up against one another screaming and crying. Cecelia did not know if the overwhelming pain she felt came from inside her own body or the crowd crushing her from the outside.

Amidst the cries and wails, Cecelia heard one girl bellow, "How did this happen—the building is fireproof!" "My little sister is still up there!" another sobbed.

But all Cecelia could think about was Rose and how she had just saved her life.

Cecelia heard her name and looked up. Joseph Zito was next to her. "I saw what Rose just did. I'll make another trip up and get her," he promised.

Still in shock, Cecelia could only nod her head.

The elevator hit the ground floor with a thud. Without a moment's hesitation, the passengers pushed their way out of the elevator and ran toward the exit.

Cecelia looked at Joseph, who had already gotten back into his elevator, ready to make yet another trip back up into the fire. But before he could do it, there was a loud snapping noise. It was almost deafening. Cecelia knew what it meant even before Joseph had a chance to tell her. The elevator cables had snapped. There was no other safe way down from the ninth floor. Rose, along with hundreds of other Triangle Shirtwaist Factory workers, was trapped in the fire raging above her. Right then and there, Cecelia knew she would never see her friend again.

6
MOVING ON

Just like on the day her father was sent to the sanatorium, Cecelia sat alone in the old storage closet. She held the journal that Rose had given her for Christmas close to her heart. It was the only thing she had left of her friend. She vowed to use it to write down her favorite memories of the times she and Rose had shared together. But today was not that day. It was too painful to think about them right now. She could still feel Rose's presence throughout the tenement, especially in the storage closet.

Cecelia put the journal down and closed her eyes. She thought about how her life had, once again, changed in an instant. Cecelia had not been back to the factory since the fire last Saturday, but she had read and heard about it everywhere. It seemed like the fire and the conditions at the Triangle Factory were all anyone in New York could talk about. "I guess those picketers outside of the Cooper Union were right," she thought. "The conditions in factories are still unsafe.

It was eight days later, and she still could not stop the images and sounds of the fire from playing over and over again in her mind. Every time Cecelia thought about Rose and what she had sacrificed for her, she could not help but tear up.

"Don't cry," Cecelia reminded herself. "Rose wouldn't want you to spend so much time wallowing. She'd want you to get up and plan how you will fulfill your American dream."

Cecelia thought about ways that she could live up to Rose's last wish. So far she had come up with nothing.

The fire only lasted less than half an hour, but its destruction was immeasurable. Of Cecelia's fellow factory workers, 146 were dead. Most of them were girls who had worked with her on the ninth floor. Even though the fire department had responded quickly, there was not much that the firemen could do to help the trapped factory workers. Like Rose saw through the window, their ladders did not reach above the sixth floor. The young men and women jumping out of the windows trying to escape the smoke and flames inside of the factory further hindered their rescue efforts.

So many questions ran through Cecelia's head. "How did the fire start? How did a building that was supposed to be modern and fireproof burn so fast? Why wasn't there a safe way out of the building?"

But no one could really answer them for her—or for anyone else. It seemed like the whole country was infuriated about the fire. The newspapers said the fire department could not determine how the fire started and probably never would. The Asch Building had all of the basic fire safety equipment, but it all failed to work. The fire escape was so flimsy that it collapsed and fell off the side of the building with workers still on it. All of them died. Even more workers jumped down the elevator chutes hoping to survive the fall. What angered Cecelia was that all of the doors that led out of the factory floor had been locked. Of course, she knew this while she was working there but didn't think anything of it before the fire.

Looking back, Cecelia couldn't help but wonder, "If the owners of the Triangle Waist Company didn't make Mrs. Lansner lock the door, would Rose and the other 145 workers still be alive? How could locking the doors so that the workers would not steal fabric scraps mean more to them than the worker's lives?" No matter how many times she tried to make sense of it, she could not. Cecelia felt hopeless.

Cecclia heard her mother softly calling her name from the hallway.

"It's time to go to church. I think you should come with me and your brothers," she said.

Although she did not really want to leave the safety and comfort of the storage closet, Cecelia thought it would be better than sitting around sulking.

"Yes, Mother. I'm coming," she replied, getting up and straightening her skirt.

Cecelia walked to Saint Anthony's with her mother and brothers. It was nice to get out. Like on the day of the fire, the weather was beautiful.

"After church, I have to go to the butcher," Lucia said. "I want to make a big dinner for when your father comes home tomorrow."

With all of the commotion about the fire and Rose's death, Cecelia had nearly forgotten that her father was better and was coming home. Mr. Costa even gave him his old job at the wine store. Of course, this also meant that Cecelia could go back to high school. She would not have to work in a garment factory ever again.

Cecelia wondered how many of the other six hundred workers who had also escaped the fire would not have to go back to work in another factory.

"Not many," she figured. She knew that, once again, luck was on her side. Cecelia empathized with these people. She did not know how they would be able to step foot inside of another factory, let alone spend twelve hours a day in one. "They are braver than I would be, that is for sure."

Just before they reached the steps of Saint Anthony's, Cecelia noticed that a crowd was gathered there. They all had roses in their hands, and they were singing Ave Maria. On the ground in front of them was a big quilt with the names of everyone—Catholic and Jewish— who died in the Triangle Shirtwaist Factory fire.

Cecelia let out a little cry. She felt sad and happy at the same time. She had not expected this outpouring of commemoration and support—especially this much sorrow for the Jewish victims. Maybe her Italian and Jewish neighbors would be more tolerant and understanding of one another now. She knew Rose would want that, too.

A stranger handed Cecelia a bright red rose as she silently walked toward the quilt of names. Cecelia couldn't help but feel comforted by this act of kindness. Even though she was still upset and knew that the terrible memories of that day would stay with her for a long time, in some small way, she knew that this was the first step toward healing. Cecelia knew that everyone was looking at her, but she didn't care. She found Rose's name on the quilt, knelt down, touched it and then placed her rose on top. Others followed her lead. Soon, roses covered every name on the quilt.

"A rose will protect each one of these fire victims just like my Rose protected me," Cecelia observed.

Cecelia felt a hand graze her back. It was in the exact spot on her back where Rose had pushed her to safety during the fire. The all-too-familiar sensation made Cecelia jump. She turned around to see who was there. When Cecelia saw the girl staring back at her, she turned as white as a ghost.

"Cecelia!" the girl cried out as she threw her arms around Cecelia's neck. "I thought I'd never see you again!" It took Cecelia a minute to realize the girl was speaking in Italian.

"Gemma, what are you doing here?" marveled Cecilia. She could not believe that her old friend was standing next to her in New York City. The last time she saw her was back in Italy. She thought about all of the time she spent wishing Gemma was with her in New York. The last time she had truly missed Gemma was before she met Rose. It seemed like a lifetime ago. Yet Gemma was here now, and it made Cecelia smile.

"I wrote to you to tell you we were coming. Didn't you get my letter?" Gemma asked.

"No," replied Cecelia. "But I'm glad I didn't get it. Seeing you here right now is a wonderful surprise!"

"I heard about your friend Rose," Gemma added. "I am so sorry, Cecelia."

"Thank you, Gemma. You and Rose would have been best of friends," mused Cecelia.

Cecelia's mother let her skip church that day. She spent the time showing Gemma around her new neighborhood. Gemma's tenement was only two blocks away. Speaking to Gemma in Italian, Cecelia pointed out her favorite things around the Lower East Side. Pretty soon, they were standing in front of Cecelia's tenement on East Seventh Street.

"Come on, I have to show you my favorite place in all of New York City," Cecelia exclaimed as she took Gemma's hand and led her to the old storage closet.

Cecelia opened the door to the room where she and Rose had spent so much time together and stepped inside. Tears welled up in her eyes. The tears were for Rose, but this time they were tears of happiness.

"This is where I am going to fulfill my American dream for both of us, Rose," Cecelia realized. "This is where I am going to teach Gemma to speak English and where I will study to become a real teacher. I will to do it for us, Rose. I will do it in your memory, knowing that you will be standing beside me the entire time."

HISTORICAL NOTE AND PHOTOS

On March 25, 1911, a fire at the Triangle Shirtwaist Factory killed 146 people. Most of these people were young girls. Up until the terror attacks of September 11, 2001, the Triangle Shirtwaist Factory fire was the worst disaster in New York City history. Working conditions in factories like the Triangle were very unsafe. The hours were long, and the pay was little. Thanks to the efforts of people like Carla Lemlich and groups like the International Ladies' Garment Workers' Union, there are now laws in place to protect workers' rights.

While the character of Cecelia Napoli is a work of fiction, many things in this book are true. The descriptions of the living conditions in the tenements, immigrant life in early New York City, the Triangle Waist Company (commonly referred to as the Triangle Shirtwaist Factory), its location and layout and the account of the fire are all based on fact.

Although not much is known about the real Rose Mehl, we do know that she was one of the youngest victims of the Triangle Shirtwaist Factory fire at fifteen years old. She was born in the United States in 1896 to Jewish immigrants. She lived in a tenement at 278 East Seventh Street, much like the one in the story. Rose is buried in Mount Zion Cemetery in Queens, New York.

A forelady on the ninth floor named Fannie Lansner and a sewing machine operator named Jennie Lederman both died in the fire, too. I like to think that, like Rose, they really did help some of their fellow workers make it out alive. One person who we know was a true hero during the fire was elevator operator Joseph Zito. He rescued over one hundred girls that day by bringing the elevator back up to the floors that were on fire until the cables snapped right before his third trip.

The Triangle Waist Company's owners, Max Blanck and Isaac Harris, were in the building when the fire started; they both survived by fleeing to the building's roof as soon as the fire began. The public outcry and pressure from unions forced city officials to put Blanck and Harris on trial. However, a jury did not find them guilty, but a few years later, they lost a civil suit and had to pay the families of every victim seventy-five dollars.

Since most of the 146 victims were immigrant women and girls from Eastern Europe, Russia and Italy, many of their families lacked the means and communication skills necessary to identify their loved ones' remains. Up until February 2011, almost one hundred years after the fire, six of the victims had not been identified.

The tragedy at the Triangle Shirtwaist Factory led to the reform of New York State labor codes, as well as fire safety measures that served as a model for the rest of the United States. Many of these codes still protect people to this day. Hopefully, the changes that arose from the ashes of the tragedy will continue to save people, the same way Rose saved Cecelia.

Immigrants being processed at Ellis Island. *Courtesy of the Library of Congress.*

Tenement buildings in the Lower East Side, New York. *Courtesy of the Library of Congress.*

A peddler with his pushcart selling his goods in the Lower East Side. *Courtesy of the Library of Congress.*

A typical kitchen in a Lower East Side tenement. *Courtesy of the Library of Congress.*

Children bathing in a tenement's kitchen sink. *Courtesy of the Library of Congress.*

Tenants evicted from their Lower East Side tenement. *Courtesy of the Library of Congress.*

Young Italian peddlers. *Courtesy of the Library of Congress.*

A busy Lower East Side street. *Courtesy of the Library of Congress.*

COPYRIGHT 1907
BY DETROIT PHOTOGRAPH

Fifth Avenue—where wealthy New Yorkers shopped. *Courtesy of the Library of Congress.*

A young immigrant girl keeps busy in a New York City tenement. *Courtesy of the Library of Congress.*

A young garment factory worker. *Courtesy of the Kheel Center, Cornell University.*

Women on the picket line. *Courtesy of the Library of Congress.*

Carla Lemlich, wearing a shirtwaist, 1909. *Courtesy of the Kheel Center, Cornell University.*

The Asch Building, home of the Triangle Waist Company, before the fire.
Courtesy of the Kheel Center, Cornell University.

Rows of sewing stations like the ones in the Triangle Shirtwaist Factory. *Courtesy of the Library of Congress.*

Garment factory sewing machine operators hard at work. *Courtesy of the Kheel Center, Cornell University.*

Max Blanck and Isaac Harris—the owners of the Triangle Shirtwaist Factory.
Courtesy of the Kheel Center, Cornell University.

The Triangle Shirtwaist Factory in flames. *Courtesy of the Kheel Center, Cornell University.*

Opposite, top: Horse-drawn FDNY fire engines raced to the Asch Building minutes after the fire began. *Courtesy of the Library of Congress.*

Opposite, bottom: The FDNY arrived to the Asch Building on time, but their ladders and hoses could not reach the fire. *Courtesy of the Kheel Center, Cornell University.*

The rickety fire escape collapsed during the fire. *Courtesy of the Kheel Center, Cornell University.*

All that remained of the Triangle Shirtwaist Factory after the fire claimed the lives of 146 workers—most of whom were young girls. *Courtesy of the Kheel Center, Cornell University.*

Firemen survey the devastation after the fire at the Triangle Shirtwaist Factory. *Courtesy of the Library of Congress.*

83

Left: Joseph Zito, an Asch Building elevator operator and Triangle Shirtwaist Factory fire hero. *Courtesy of the Kheel Center, Cornell University.*

Below: The March 28, 1911 *New York Evening Journal's* coverage of the tragedy. *Courtesy of the Kheel Center, Cornell University.*

A New York City Italian newspaper headlined the tragedy at the Triangle
Shirtwaist Factory on March 26, 1911. *Courtesy of the Library of Congress.*

Index

DISCUSSION QUESTIONS

• What were some of the biggest obstacles immigrants faced when coming to the United States? Give specific examples of the hardships Cecelia faced when coming to New York.

• Discuss the different cultures of people who came to New York and how these cultures shaped the United States as it is today.

• Discuss the ways that labor laws have changed since the early 1900s, as well as the impact Carla Lemlich had on these changes.

• Explain why Rose and Cecelia were afraid to tell their parents about their friendship.

• How does Cecelia describe the conditions in the tenements? Discuss the features of these neighborhoods and living conditions. Could you ever live in a tenement? Why or why not?

• When Cecelia's father contracted consumption, he was sent to a sanatorium. How did sickness and disease impact the tenement housing and the families living there?

• Cecelia talks about Rose having "perfect English." Describe the ways in which learning more than one language (especially English) was important to immigrants.

• Cecelia and Rose talk about the different types of meals they share with their family. Discuss the ways in which different cultures celebrate holidays and specific traditions with food and family.

• Why do you think immigrants like Lorenzo Napoli were prejudiced toward other immigrant groups? List an example of how this type of prejudice still exists in today's society.

• Discuss what the American dream meant for many of the immigrants coming to New York. Why do you think Cecelia and Rose focused on work so much, even during their free time?

• What are some of the difficult working conditions that people faced in factories? Why do you think factory workers like Cecelia and Rose ignored how dangerous these conditions were?

• Why do you think Rose and Cecelia became such good friends? What does each girl gain from the friendship?

• Discuss the ways technology has changed the way old businesses like the Triangle Waist Company operate. How do modern American companies differ from companies in the early 1900s?

• Explain the significance of Ellis Island in America's history, as well as its importance to the individuals who arrived there and to future generations in their family lines.

• Rose asks Cecelia to go to a nickelodeon. What is a nickelodeon? How does it differ from modern-day weekend activities?

• How did the people who lived on Fifth Avenue differ from the people living in the Lower East Side in the early 1900s? Do you think they had similar American dreams? Why or why not?

• Why did Rose push Cecelia into the elevator instead of trying to save her own life? How does Cecelia honor her friend's memory?

• List five reasons why immigrants chose to suffer a long journey to a foreign land and brutal housing conditions to live in the United States.

• Discuss the differences between Cecelia's and Rose's household roles. How are they different? How are they similar?

• Why was education so important to both Cecelia and Rose?

• Cecelia's mother tells her she resembles "a real Lady Liberty." What did the Statue of Liberty represent to immigrants coming to a new country?

• Discuss the significance of community while living in the tenements in the early 1900s. What were some important features of a strong community? Why did both Cecelia's and Rose's families have strong opinions about both their own and other communities in the Lower East Side?

• What are some of the ways the owners of the Triangle Shirtwaist Factory could have made the workplace safer for their workers? Discuss how the author used foreshadowing to give clues about how the fire happened.

• Do you think a tragedy like the fire at the Triangle Shirtwaist Factory could happen today? Why or why not?

• Although 146 people died under their watch, the owners of the Triangle Shirtwaist Factory were not held responsible. Do you think this was fair or unfair? Why?

About the Author

Mary Kate Doman has written over twenty books for young readers. When she is not writing, Mary Kate consults for some of the biggest children's and young adult imprints and publishing houses around the world. She also teaches children's publishing and literature classes at the graduate level.

Mary Kate lives with her husband, Tim, and their daughter, Tess (who was born while Mary Kate was writing this book), in Brooklyn.

You can visit her online at www.MaryKateDoman.com.